"Sometimes people forget that you're a human being, and that you're no different than any other mortal."

— Jesse Owens, American athlete

Zeus, king of the Greek gods, in whose honor the first Olympic games were held

Lives OF THE Athletes

THRILLS, SPILLS

(and What the Neighbors Thought)

❧≈✦≈❧

WRITTEN BY KATHLEEN KRULL

ILLUSTRATED BY KATHRYN HEWITT

HARCOURT BRACE & COMPANY

SAN DIEGO   NEW YORK   LONDON

I am indebted to the Harcourt Brace sales force;
Rubin Pfeffer, Jeannette Larson, Coy Batson, Susan Cohen;
Kathryn, David, and Paul Hewitt; Kenneth O. and Kenneth M. Krull;
Pat Riddle, Larry Dane Brimner, Tony Johnston; the Volleyball Hall of Fame,
United States Volleyball Association, the Hockey Hall of Fame, and
Preston Levi at the International Swimming Hall of Fame.
—K. K.

Special thanks to Shirley Ito at the
Amateur Athletic Foundation of Los Angeles, California
—K. H.

Library of Congress Cataloging-in-Publication Data
Krull, Kathleen.
Lives of the athletes: thrills, spills (and what the neighbors thought)/
by Kathleen Krull; illustrated by Kathryn Hewitt.
p. cm.
Includes bibliographical references.
Summary: Presents twenty true stories of athletes—mostly admirable, occasionally quirky—
whose physical accomplishments create a world of thrills and spills.
ISBN 0-15-200806-3
ISBN 0-8172-4191-4 library binding
1. Athletes—Biography—Juvenile literature. [1. Athletes.]
I. Hewitt, Kathryn, ill.   II. Title.
GV697.A1K78   1997
796'.092'2—dc20   95-50702
[B]

C E G F D
PRINTED IN SINGAPORE

The illustrations in this book were done in watercolor and colored pencil on watercolor paper.
The display type was set in Colwell.
The text type was set in Goudy by Thompson Type, San Diego, California.
Color separations by Bright Arts, Ltd., Singapore
Printed and bound by Tien Wah Press, Singapore
This book was printed on totally chlorine-free Nymolla Matte Art paper.
Production supervision by Stanley Redfern
Designed by Lisa Peters and Linda Lockowitz

To Kathryn Hewitt,

the inspiration for the Lives of . . . *books,*

for her grace and energy

—K. K.

To Paul, a smart jock

—K. H.

Contents

Introduction

THROUGHOUT HISTORY, those who practice the art of the human body have inspired us with superhuman feats. Pushing themselves past their limits, they have climbed the highest mountains (Hillary), swum the most dangerous oceans (Ederle), surfed the biggest waves (Kahanamoku), and broken the toughest barriers (Robinson). In striving for physical perfection, athletes have caused riots, earned enormous sums of money, and influenced entire generations. But what were they like as people? Were their actions in private always so sportsmanlike? And were they as popular with their neighbors as with their fans?

The life of an athlete is surely intense—some have even perished while playing their sport (Maravich, Hyman). Athletes have been snubbed by world leaders (Owens) and congratulated by one out of every ten of their countrymen (Clemente). They have imperiled themselves by chasing thieves down alleys (Henie) and roared at the most inappropriate times (Weissmuller).

Neighbors can make an athlete's life even more intense. Some neighbors have been tough enough to make martial arts a requirement for survival (Lee) or intrusive enough to dictate protective measures (Pelé). Neighbors have gotten together to help Olympic-bound competitors (Rudolph) and have cherished an athlete's almost saintly presence (Ashe). On the other hand, wild parties can be annoying to neighboring farmers (Ruth), and some neighbors do regret the sacrifice of their entire marble collections (Zaharias). Steak has with unusual frequency been the breakfast of champions, though at least one champion has been famous among neighbors for stews of fresh fish or raccoon (Thorpe).

Whatever their appetites, or whoever their neighbors, the athletic stars who excite us today sometimes exceed the records of their predecessors. But this has not decreased our fascination with legendary role models and their exploits. Here are twenty true stories of athletes—mostly admirable, occasionally quirky—offered as a celebration of physical accomplishment that transports us into a world of thrills and spills.

—Kathleen Krull

Jim Thorpe

BORN IN PRAGUE, OKLAHOMA, 1888
DIED IN LOMITA, CALIFORNIA, 1953

A Sauk and Fox Indian, hero of the
1912 Olympics, considered by many to be the best
all-around athlete in American history

JAMES FRANCIS THORPE's tribal name was Wa-tho-huck, which means "Bright Path." "I cannot decide," he once said, "whether I was well named or not. Many a time the path has gleamed bright for me, but just as often it has been dark and bitter indeed."

Between the ages of seven and sixteen, he was grieved by the deaths of his twin brother, mother, and father. Unhappy within classroom walls of government schools on the reservation, he worked on ranches instead, fixing fences and catching and saddling wild horses. His family tried to make it harder for him to run away by sending him to schools farther and farther from home.

He finally found contentment at the Carlisle Indian School in Pennsylvania, where he began breaking the school's athletic records. He excelled at football, basketball (he was captain of the team and played all positions), and everything else, including dancing (he won the two-step contest). One summer he played baseball for fifteen dollars a week to pick up extra money. At Christmas he put on a Santa Claus suit and handed out toys to the younger schoolchildren.

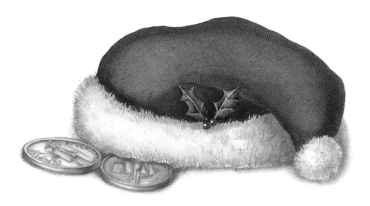

At age twenty-four, Thorpe made it to Sweden to compete in the Olympics, thrilling thirty thousand spectators with his track-and-field performance. President William Taft sent a letter congratulating him on "those qualities which characterize the best type of American citizenship." Ironically, it was not for another twelve years that Thorpe or any Indian was in fact granted citizenship. All his life Thorpe—a true hero to all tribes—campaigned for equal rights for Indians.

A year after the Olympics, however, a reporter dug up the information that Thorpe had long ago been paid for playing baseball, a technicality that disqualified him from Olympic competition. He was forced to turn over his gold medals to the second-place winners. This blow was followed four years later by the death of Jim Jr., his baby son. Friends said Thorpe never fully recovered from the loss, and he began to drink heavily.

His wife at the time had been a fellow Carlisle student, Iva Miller, with whom he went on to have three daughters—Gail, Charlotte, and Grace. With his second wife, Freeda Kirkpatrick, he had four sons—Carl Phillip, William, Richard, and John. His third wife, Patricia Askew, acted as his manager and convinced him to accept fees for his increasingly frequent speeches around the country. She pointed out that his fabled generosity—he always picked up hitchhikers, never failed to accommodate a friend, and sold the rights to his life story (which became a hit movie) for a small sum—still gave him "two-way pockets."

Easygoing and a ready listener, Thorpe was well liked for his integrity and his gentle ways. He took his sons hunting for raccoons and rabbits and was a good cook, famous among neighbors for stews of raccoon or fish. He loved raising dogs and had as many as eighteen in the backyards of his cottages and trailers. The only thing known to make him mad was racial prejudice; once during a baseball game a manager called him a "dumb Indian" and Thorpe tackled him on the spot. He never spoke of his lost Olympic medals.

Thorpe was voted into three sports' Halls of Fame and won (by a landslide) a poll to recognize the Greatest Athlete of the Half-Century. He died after his third heart attack, at age sixty-four, while eating lunch in his trailer.

Thirty years later, after constant petitions by groups who thought the taking of his gold medals was unfair and motivated by racism, the decision was finally reversed. Much paperwork later, the medals were again presented—in a ceremony attended by six of Thorpe's children.

Athleticisms

➤ Thorpe and the rest of the Carlisle football team didn't think they stood a chance against the U.S. Military Academy at West Point, a much more accomplished team. Then the Carlisle coach reminded the team that the fathers and grandfathers of the West Point players made up the army that had fought and defeated the Indians. Carlisle won the game, 27 to 6. Playing for West Point that day was Dwight Eisenhower, future president of the United States, who noted of Thorpe that "on the football field there was no one like him in the world."

➤ Thorpe's Olympic triumph consisted of the fifteen grueling events that make up the pentathlon and decathlon, regarded as the ultimate tests of physical strength. Presenting him with his two gold medals, the king of Sweden was moved to say, "Sir, you are the greatest athlete in the world." Newspapers reported Thorpe's simple response: "Thanks, King."

UP TO HIS NECK IN FLOWERS

Duke Kahanamoku

BORN IN 1890 AND DIED IN 1968
IN HONOLULU, HAWAII

Legendary Hawaiian swimmer and surfer,
credited with introducing surfing around the world

NON-HAWAIIANS had trouble saying the long last name—Ka-ha-na-mo-ku—but loved the first one. It wasn't a royal title but the name of his father, one of numerous babies named Duke in honor of a visit to the islands by the British Duke of Edinburgh. All the Kahanamoku males were outstanding swimmers and surfers, but it was Duke Jr. who brought Hawaii into the world spotlight with his swimming medals at the 1912 and 1920 Olympics. In a case of rare longevity, he also competed in the 1924 Olympics and even tried out in 1928 and 1932, making the water polo team at age forty-two.

Kahanamoku spent most of his youth in the ocean and dropped out of high school after one year. Thus, in between Olympics, his limited education made it difficult and sometimes humiliating for him to make a living. He did all sorts of odd jobs, but his salvation turned out to be movies. Appearing in some thirty films (in various "ethnic" roles) forced him to stay on the mainland for long spells but supplied steady income.

Women fell all over Kahanamoku—he took them surfing and on romantic moonlit horseback rides—but his lack of financial security kept him from

15

marrying until he was almost fifty. Then he and Nadine Alexander, a ballet and ballroom dance teacher, lived in a beach house where he had a koa wood bed custom-made to fit his large body.

Kahanamoku carried himself regally and, without seeking it, was invariably the center of attention wherever he went. Everyone he met came away respecting his dignity, courage, and style. He had an excellent memory for names and faces, a good sense of humor, and a reputation as a reporter's nightmare because he was pleasant but very private—"I guess I'm the scarcest talker I ever met." (The movies he made were mostly silent ones.) Once at a reception honoring him, he admitted that he wasn't a good speaker, "but in the water I'll do my best to please everybody"—which was a long speech for him. One of the last of the full-blooded Polynesians native to Hawaii, he was beloved throughout the islands. Whenever he returned from a trip, he was greeted with lei piled so high around his neck that his face barely peeped out of the fresh Hawaiian flowers. His superhero reputation increased after a boating accident, when he went out on his surfboard and single-handedly rescued eight drowning people.

Eventually he was elected as sheriff of Honolulu and held the job for twenty-six years. He improved jail conditions and later was named Hawaii's Official Greeter. The tourism his feats inspired brought enormous change to Hawaii; his boyhood home and hangouts were replaced by fancy hotels and high-rises.

A charter member of the Swimming Hall of Fame and the Surfing Hall of Fame, Kahanamoku surfed well into his sixties. At his sixtieth birthday party, he personally served each of the five hundred guests a slice of cake. Ten thousand people were invited to his seventy-seventh birthday party, where he was given a new car with a hood ornament of a gold-plated statue of himself surfing and license plates that read DUKE. Five months later he died after a heart attack at the Waikiki Yacht Club, where he had been helping friends repaint boats and riding in his own new powerboat. His ashes were scattered over the side of one of the canoes in a flotilla on the Pacific, followed by so many bright lei that the surrounding ocean became a carpet of orchids and carnations.

Athleticisms

>>> Kahanamoku first came to the public's attention at age twenty in a swimming competition. Breaking two long-standing world records turned the talented local beachboy into a world-renowned swimmer. To him winning was secondary—he just loved to swim, and he found it painful to embarrass an opponent. His coaches had to push him to focus on winning—he swam fast enough to *just* beat whoever came in second.

>>> Surfing, a sport formerly reserved for Hawaiian kings, was closely linked with religious ceremonies and prayers. It flared into general popularity after Kahanamoku put on spectacular shows of his surfing skill. He liked surfing more than swimming and once made what has been called the greatest ride in surfing history. Cruising waves so huge they could have killed him (as high as thirty feet) for one and three-quarters miles, he coasted past the cheering crowds that had gathered on shore.

THE POWER OF PICKLED EELS

Babe Ruth

BORN IN BALTIMORE, MARYLAND, 1895
DIED IN NEW YORK CITY, 1948

*Considered the best player
in American baseball history, most famous
for hitting more than seven hundred home runs*

EVERYTHING ABOUT George Herman Ruth's life was dramatic, even his childhood. Between the ages of seven and twenty, he lived at St. Mary's Industrial School for Boys, a training school for boys whose parents couldn't take care of them. No one knows why he was placed there—he said vaguely, "I was a bad kid"—but it's possible he refused to attend school or was getting into trouble that his parents, who worked long hours in a bar, couldn't handle. After his mother died and he stopped getting company on Sunday, Ruth would say, "I guess I'm too big and ugly to have visitors." Ruth worked in the school's factory making shirts, specializing in collars. "I had a rotten start," he once concluded.

With its eight hundred boys, however, the school did have forty baseball teams organized at various age levels, and early on a teacher steered Ruth into the game. He became the undisputed star of St. Mary's and always credited Brother Matthias with keeping him out of jail. The last notation for Ruth in the school's ledger read: "He is going to join the Balt. Baseball Team."

Ruth took his first train ride on his way to join the minor leagues. He spent his first pocket money bribing a hotel elevator operator to let him go up and down numerous times; with his first paycheck he bought his own bicycle; and with his first substantial check he bought a new bar for his father to run and personally helped him set up the business. Within a year of leaving his sheltered life at St. Mary's, Ruth was a successful professional athlete, well traveled, and rolling in money. He also acquired a permanent nickname from being constantly referred to as the newest baby or *babe* (latest discovery) of his team's owner.

As Ruth went on to become the top attraction in baseball history, people would go home laughing after his games, giddy from sharing his sensational performances. In trying to explain his strategy, he said, "I swing big, with everything I've got. I hit big or I miss big. I like to live as big as I can." Fans thought of him as a big hero—not just an athlete but a mythic figure.

Stories sprang up about every last detail of his life, even his meals. People talked about the pickled eels made by teammate Lou Gehrig's mother—Ruth ate them with chocolate ice cream between games. His usual pregame lunch was a glass of bicarbonate of soda, to settle his stomach from the several hot dogs he washed down with it. Once Ruth was hospitalized for seven weeks following surgery for indigestion—"the bellyache heard round the world," according to newspapers—said to be caused by a meal of twelve hot dogs and eight bottles of soda. He amazed companions with his wide throat—he could drink a glass of liquid in one swallow, including whole ice cubes. He didn't mind his reputation for grossness and sometimes overate just to add to the legend—ordering six sandwiches at a time or omelets made from eighteen eggs (with six slices of buttered toast and three chunks of ham on the side).

Ruth had favorite restaurants in every city, and he was always chewing, whether it was food, gum, or tobacco (he picked up the tobacco habit at age seven). He smoked cigars, cigarettes, and pipes. He had a stupendous belch, and won one of his trophies in a contest for making other digestive noises.

Lake View Public Library

Mitch W. Frank   7-01-2005
     1313   5:15 PM

Materials Being Checked Out:

    19918 Santa clause
          Due Date: 7-08-05   11:59 PM
    42267 new kid at school /
          Due Date: 7-15-05   11:59 PM
    29822 Lives of the Athletes : Thri
          Due Date: 7-15-05   11:59 PM
_____

Materials Currently Checked Out:

    41585 Niagara Falls, or do
          Due Date: 7-08-05   11:59 PM
    19918 The Santa clause
          Due Date: 7-01-05   11:59 PM
    41669 Extraordinary Healin
          Due Date: 7-08-05   11:59 PM
    42171 50 Ways to Paint a W
          Due Date: 7-08-05   11:59 PM
_____

Some thought him "the most selfish and inconsiderate man ever to put on a baseball uniform." Others believed he was one of those people who made life more fun—he was casual, warm, exuberant, "a constant source of joy." Someone once called him "the most uninhibited human being I have ever known," for his earthiness and occasional crudeness. To President Warren Harding on a boiling day at the ballpark, he said, "Hot as hell, ain't it, Prez?" At a formal dinner party, he announced in suave tones that he wasn't going to partake of the fancy asparagus salad because "asparagus makes my urine smell."

Ruth negotiated his own baseball contracts and drove a hard bargain. At his peak he made $80,000 a year, a kingly sum—the next highest paid player was making $17,500, and even President Herbert Hoover made only $75,000. (Ruth commented, "Why not? I had a better year than he did.") He bought a large new car every year, usually a Cadillac, which he drove fast, not fussy about speed limits and traffic signals. In general he didn't like authority and did what he wanted, which made him the idol of others who wanted to break rules and still be champions. He could lose his temper royally but seldom stayed angry long— "I'm hotheaded," he would say by way of apology.

A generous tipper, Ruth would give a $100 bill to someone who simply delivered him a ham sandwich. He bought diamonds for women he hardly knew, and if a celebration party lacked a piano, he bought one. He frequently visited children in hospitals and orphanages—partly for good public relations, but also because he genuinely loved kids. His visits with children were often the only times he seemed truly at ease. In a famous episode, he met Johnny Sylvester, an eleven-year-old badly hurt in a fall from a horse; embroidered versions of the story have Johnny miraculously recovering after Ruth hit a home run for him.

Worshipful crowds followed Ruth wherever he went. He adored nightlife and could party all night and still play well the next day. Legendary for seldom changing his underwear and even (it was rumored) for not wearing any, he lounged around his elegant hotel suites in a red robe and red slippers. He loved to sing and had a rich, booming voice. With a notoriously bad memory for faces and names, including those of his own teammates, he called older women Mom, older men Pop, and all other men Doc or Keed (for Kid). When he went hunting, he took along a phonograph and fifty records so he could rough it in style. One of his favorite activities was hunting frogs at night; he considered a good catch an omen for hits in the next game.

Ruth's first wife was Helen, a waitress. With their daughter, Dorothy, they eventually moved to an eighty-acre farm outside Boston, which they named Home Plate. He decorated the house by nailing baseball souvenirs to the walls. He tried to fit into the rural lifestyle, with his collie named Dixie and twenty head of cattle, but neighboring farmers did not appreciate his wild parties.

Ruth bought Helen lavish gifts, like $5,000 fur coats, but also frequently spent nights elsewhere. Three months after Helen died in a fire, he married Claire, a model, and adopted her daughter Julia. Claire became his manager, persuading him to save money instead of spending it as fast as he could, and to stop wearing garish clothes and start buying debonair suits by the dozen. She tried to improve his diet, too, and introduced him to orange juice.

Ruth died of throat cancer at age fifty-three, two months after his last appearance in a baseball uniform (to acknowledge a standing ovation at the twenty-fifth anniversary of Yankee Stadium, known as the House That Ruth Built). His grave still draws constant visitors, and in 1995 his name and likeness generated more than $25 million in retail sales.

Athleticisms

➤ During his career as a New York Yankee, Ruth hit more than seven hundred home runs at a time when home runs were rare. Before a game he'd say, "I feel hitterish today," but was modest and thought of his skill as a gift. The record of which he was most proud he set as a pitcher: twenty-nine scoreless innings in a row, a record that stood for forty-two years.

➤ Both a hypochondriac and a ham, Ruth could play well when he was injured. Every time he was hospitalized, rumors of his death surged; "I feel pretty good for a dead man," he would say. Once he was in the hospital for a week in serious condition, with acute swelling of the larynx and a high fever. A week after his release, he hit four home runs in four straight games. Another time, going after a ball, he crashed into a chicken-wire fence and cut his finger badly enough to rip the nail off. He limped off the field (though his legs had not been hurt) and made a fuss, but the next day played well, bandaged hand and all.

➤ Ruth's most thrilling home runs were ones he seemed to indicate in advance, a nearly impossible exploit that fit his flair for drama. Most famous was the home run in Chicago during the 1932 World Series, when hostile Cubs fans spit on him as he entered his hotel. On the field, while most spectators booed and threw lemons, Ruth cheerfully picked the lemons up and threw them back. Then he proceeded—or so many people swear—to point to a spot and hit a home run precisely there. "I never had so much fun in all my life," Ruth said later.

Red Grange

BORN IN FORKSVILLE, PENNSYLVANIA, 1903
DIED IN INDIAN LAKE ESTATES, FLORIDA, 1991

*Electrifying football player
often credited with single-handedly
popularizing the sport*

HAROLD EDWARD GRANGE, known as Red for his flaming red hair, hated school and wanted to quit. But his father persuaded him to remain so he could pursue sports, and Grange obliged by becoming the most publicized high school athlete in Illinois, starring in football, basketball, baseball, and track. For eight summers he also delivered blocks of ice weighing two hundred pounds, twelve hours a day; he was offered easier jobs but found that this was the ideal way to keep himself "tough as nails." He also did all the cooking for his father and brother (his mother died when he was five), as well as the housecleaning.

On the football team at the University of Illinois, his speed and elusiveness earned him an additional nickname: the Galloping Ghost. The cheering crowd and the marching bands inspired him—stirring music gave him a fighting spirit.

Twenty-four hours after turning in his well-worn college jersey, Grange became professional football's first $100,000-a-year player—at a time when the average pay was $25 a game. In those days many thought that playing sports for money was a huge mistake, but Grange didn't see anything wrong with getting paid such a sum and never regretted his decision. With his first paycheck, he bought a car for his brother, gave his dad a check for $1,000, and treated himself to a big raccoon coat. He bought the three of them a large house and furnished it by way of the Marshall Field department store. He built a four-car garage with its own gas pump and every possible tool—he loved working on cars.

Grange was famous for uncommon humility. Quick to praise teammates, he felt that people blew his own accomplishments out of proportion—though he appreciated the compliments and only protested when they got facts wrong, like saying he had big feet (he was rather proud of his size nines). No one was ever known to say anything negative about his behavior on or off the field. As elusive with fans as with opponents, he was always trying to slip away after big games, often to go to the movies.

After Grange retired from football at age thirty-one, he worked harder than ever—as an insurance company executive, doing play-by-play accounts of football games every week on radio and TV (an estimated 480 games in all), and

speaking at as many as fifty football banquets a year. He appeared in several silent movies, including a series of high-action thrillers called *The Galloping Ghost*, in which he did almost all of his own stunts. At forty-eight he had a heart attack (and was embarrassed to be carried out of his Chicago apartment on a stretcher) and afterward scaled back his activities. He settled into a white ranch house he designed himself in Indian Lake Estates, Florida, with its own orange grove, indoor swimming pool, and backyard lagoon. There he fished, tried to make friends with baby alligators in the lagoon, and fed wildlife—quail, rabbits, cranes. "I've been footballed up to my eyeballs," he joked once to explain why he was mowing the lawn instead of watching the Super Bowl.

Grange met Margaret Hazelberg, a flight attendant and his future wife, on a plane; he got her phone number by promising her football tickets. She called him Honey; he called her Muggs and "the finest 'manager' a man could have." He died of pneumonia at eighty-seven, a few months before their fiftieth wedding anniversary.

Athleticisms

➤➤ In 1924, in what is still regarded as the greatest one-man show of college football, Grange scored four touchdowns in the first twelve minutes of a game against the undefeated Michigan Wolverines. It was a hot Indian summer day, and the Illinois coach had ordered his players to strip off their customary heavy wool stockings. Always modest, Grange credited the day's victory to the confusion caused by the first sockless game in history.

➤➤ When he made his debut with the Chicago Bears, Grange had become such a figure of legend that the game drew the largest turnout for football thus far. In his first season he played as many as eight games in eleven days and, as he said, "there wasn't a bone in my body that didn't ache like the devil." But because of him, football stories that had previously been buried on the third page of the sports section now moved to the front page, and after 1925 the sport grew steadily more popular.

Johnny Weissmuller

BORN IN WINDBER, PENNSYLVANIA, 1904
DIED IN ACAPULCO, MEXICO, 1984

Record-breaking American swimmer,
winner of five gold medals at the 1924 and
1928 Olympics, later famous as Tarzan

AS A CHILD Johnny Weissmuller was so small and weak that he was put on a special diet and urged to swim to build himself up. In exchange for some of his mother's apple strudel, lifeguards let him swim day or night. When his coach promised him a steak dinner every time he broke a record, Weissmuller proceeded to eat steak at least fifty-one times. For ten years he not only held all the records but never lost a race, bringing glamour to a sport once considered dull. For luck he always touched wood before jumping into the water; it was hard to find trees near a pool, so he wore a ring made of wood.

Weissmuller was outgoing, untemperamental, and carefree. His motto was "Le's go!" He liked fast cars, especially his Buick with the leopard-skin top, but otherwise had simple tastes. He enjoyed hanging around with lifeguards more than going to fancy parties, where the champagne bubbles would make him sneeze. In later life, when he wasn't so skinny, he sometimes went to weight-loss clinics, where the regime was a glass of lemon juice in the morning and three lean meals. Careless with money, he sometimes did not even read contracts before he signed them.

Women loved Weissmuller. He liked them, too, and married five: Bobbe Arnst, a nightclub singer (on their first date, they went swimming); Lupe Velez, a Mexican actress (when they were dating, he'd visit her mainly to swim in her pool, calling "Hi, Lupe!" on his way in); Beryel Scott, a golfer with whom he had three children (John Jr., Wendy, and Heidi); Allene Gates, another golfer he offered to give swimming lessons to when he found out she couldn't swim; and Maria Bauman, a German aristocrat. He lived in a Spanish-style mansion on Rodeo Drive in Beverly Hills, and later in Las Vegas and Mexico. Wherever he lived, he had a pool and took a dip every day.

Weissmuller fell into a second glamorous career when Hollywood scouts were hunting for someone to star in *Tarzan of the Apes*, based on Edgar Rice Burroughs's series about an English lord marooned in Africa. Weissmuller, then modeling for an underwear company, passed an audition that consisted of climbing a tree, taking off his clothes, and carrying a woman. He went on to appear in

nineteen Tarzan films, looking good in a leopard-skin loincloth, making five thousand dollars a week, performing his own stunts, and befriending the lions and chimpanzees he worked with (though getting constant tetanus shots because they often scratched him accidentally). Sometimes friends joked that they didn't recognize him with his clothes on; in his later TV series, *Jungle Jim*, he did wear clothes.

With the powerful lungs he'd developed from swimming, Weissmuller came up with Tarzan's famous chest-thumping roar in homage to the yodeling contests at Austrian-German picnics he'd attended as a child. Once, when he was in Cuba and found the road blocked by armed revolutionaries, he did the yell, and the rebels recognized him and escorted him to safety. Another time, while hospitalized, he yelled in the middle of the night, terrifying the other patients.

"Old Tarzans never die," Weissmuller would say, still a spectacular swimmer into his late sixties. But he failed to survive a series of strokes he had at age seventy-nine, a few miles from the lake where his last movie was shot. As his casket was lowered into the ground, friends played a tape of the trademark Tarzan cry.

Athleticisms

➤ In the middle of the 1924 Olympics, Weissmuller and another swimmer spontaneously put on a comical swimming and diving act that drove the crowd wild with enthusiasm. Officials were less amused and banned similar interruptions at future Olympics. Weissmuller went on to win three gold medals, setting three world records. Many thought he had a gift for comedy and could have had a second career as a comedian instead of as Tarzan.

➤ Just before the 1928 Olympics, Weissmuller pulled a tendon in his leg but didn't tell anyone for fear of being told he couldn't race. It got worse, and when he finally sought treatment, his leg healed in time for him to go on to win two gold medals. The lesson he took from this was the importance of focusing on his goal, which was winning, not covering up injuries just so he could compete.

"WHAT FOR?"

Gertrude Ederle

Pioneering American swimmer
who created a sensation in 1926 as the first woman
to swim across the icy English Channel

GERTRUDE EDERLE grew up on liverwurst and pickles from the delicatessen her German immigrant parents owned next to their house. The girl they called Trudy made her own clothes and sewed for the younger sisters in her large family. Summers were spent at a cottage in New Jersey, where Ederle's father taught her to swim at age eight. A few years later she joined the Women's Swimming Association (WSA) on Manhattan's lower East Side. When a fellow swimmer mocked the way Ederle was attempting to learn a new stroke, she responded by making up her mind to not only beat that girl but to become a champion.

Not a time waster, Ederle became at age twelve the youngest person ever to break a world record, going on to break twenty-nine U.S. and world records in all. At the 1924 Olympics—only the second time that American women had swum in the Olympics—she took home three medals, two bronze and one gold.

Then, at age nineteen, she announced her intention to swim across the English Channel, considered the ultimate test of a swimmer's endurance. The Channel consisted of more than twenty miles of cold, choppy water, high winds, powerful

33

currents, huge freighters to watch for (this was then the busiest shipping lane in the world), bites from jellyfish and Portuguese men-of-war, and constant seasickness, fatigue, and fear.

At a time when female swimmers were usually weighed down with enough garments to sink them, Ederle made a splash with just the look of her bathing suit—a sleek, black silk one-piece embossed with a small American flag. For her swim across the Channel, she also wore three layers of protective grease: olive oil, lanolin, and lard mixed with petroleum jelly. She entered the water at 7:09 A.M.,

accompanied by a tugboat that held her coach (who cheered her on with calls of "Take it easy . . . take your time"), her father (who had promised her a little red Buick if she made it across), reporters and photographers, and a Victrola that played her favorite songs—"Yes, We Have No Bananas" and "Let Me Call You Sweetheart." After twelve hours the people in the boat were becoming seasick. Worried about Ederle's safety, they told her to quit. Ederle raised her head and, not pausing in her six-beat-per-stroke propeller-like kicks, called, "What for?" She walked on shore at 9:40 that night, smiling and laughing. When reporters asked how she felt, she replied, "Wet."

Instantly Ederle became the most famous teen in the world. Two million people joined her triumphant parade up Broadway—the largest crowd ever to turn out in New York, equaled only by that a year later for aviator Charles Lindbergh. President Calvin Coolidge named her America's Best Girl.

Ederle made appearances on stage and worked as a fashion designer, but the buffeting her head took in the Channel contributed to a gradual loss of hearing. When she later injured her spine in a fall, doctors said she would never walk again. Rather than give in to despair, she not only walked but learned to swim again and taught swimming to deaf children. She never married or had children; neighbors found her to be shy and stubborn but mostly sunny and unselfish.

Ederle not only inspired thousands of women to take to the water; she paved the way for women entering all competitive sports. In 1965 she won election to the International Swimming Hall of Fame, and in 1980 to the Women's Sports Hall of Fame.

Athleticisms

➤ Ederle's Channel crossing in 1926 was not her first attempt. The previous year she had lasted only nine hours before she had to be rescued, half-unconscious from nausea. She refused to be haunted by her failure and vowed that on her second attempt she would swim until she could not move. Her goal was not money or fame but rather to publicly thank the WSA, which she felt had done so much for her. With the first money she earned after her success, she reimbursed the WSA for what it had spent to send her to England.

➤ Before Ederle, hundreds of men and women had tried to cross the Channel and failed; only five (all men) had succeeded. Crossing was universally considered an impossible feat for a woman, but in fact Ederle's time beat the men's record by two hours. Her record stood for twenty-four years. As for the feats of more recent swimmers, Ederle's philosophy was one of encouragement: "Records are made to be broken."

Babe Didrikson Zaharias

BORN IN PORT ARTHUR, TEXAS, 1911
DIED IN GALVESTON, TEXAS, 1956

*Influential American star of golf and many
other sports, winner of three Olympic medals,
considered the greatest modern woman athlete*

AS A CHILD she owned all the neighbors' marbles because she always won, and she turned errands into exploits, jumping hedges on her way to and from the grocery store. After the day she hit five home runs in one game, like a female Babe Ruth, people seldom referred to her as Mildred (her real name) again.

Babe Didrikson Zaharias could play the harmonica, type one hundred words a minute, sew (the blue silk dress she made took first place at the Texas State Fair, and later she designed and sewed her own golf outfits), and light matches with a flick of her fingernail. She was a whiz at crossword puzzles, became a great ballroom dancer, and cooked with aplomb, specializing in meatballs as prepared by her Norwegian mother. Like a figure from a Texas tall tale, Zaharias simply did all things well.

But her true aim, as a preteen, was "to be the greatest athlete that ever lived." Besides baseball, she excelled at basketball, track, tennis, diving, bowling, golf, and almost every other game. She claimed not to have a favorite sport, liking them all: "I sleep them, eat them, talk them, and try my level best to do them as they should be done."

The star of her high school basketball team (once she joined, the team never lost a game), Zaharias attracted the attention of a scout for an insurance company. She dropped out of school and went to work as a secretary, but her real job was to star in the company's athletic program for women; the coach promised her a chocolate soda each time she jumped higher than she ever had before. She began supporting her large poor family, providing a radio, a bedroom set, an electric refrigerator and stove, a car. She bought her mother eight new dresses (one for each day of the week plus an extra for Sunday) and later paid for the education of her nieces and nephews.

Zaharias jumped her way to the Olympics. Yet even though her Olympic triumphs made her a household name, it is hard to overemphasize the stereotyping inflicted on her. During a time when women were not supposed to get sweaty, much less engage in competitive sports, Zaharias faced vicious judgments, constant rumors of lesbianism, and cruel jokes about her looks. Her appearance was always discussed before her accomplishments were; whole feature stories would be devoted to her purchase of a new hat. Zaharias was just too unusual *not* to attract attention—she was unmarried, self-supporting, and on her way to becoming a millionaire. Once, when asked about a diamond ring she was wearing, she said, "Bought it myself. It was a diamond I wanted, not a man."

With no real peers, she led a solitary life until she married a professional wrestler, George Zaharias. He called her Romance and ended his career, becoming her manager and keeping her career going. Before her golf tournaments he would sleep in a separate room because he didn't want his snoring to disturb her. He weighed more than twice as much as she did, and he grew larger—eventually weighing more than four hundred pounds. He ate sticks of butter like bananas, and their bed, eight feet square, had to be specially made. Zaharias sometimes expressed regret that they had no children, but their relationship was playful.

Even during times when they were unhappy (a tip-off was when she bought a small convertible she knew George couldn't fit into), they kept up a public image of true romance. They were often apart but ran up huge phone bills talking to each other.

Zaharias sometimes got nervous in front of crowds—her stomach so jumpy that it visibly moved—but she also loved the goosebumps that crowds gave her. The bigger the crowd, the more she liked it. When she was around, reporters sharpened their pencils and photographers brought extra film. They relished her

refreshing honesty, her flamboyant sense of humor, and her extraordinary self-confidence—which at the time was expected in a man but was front-page news in a woman. Exaggerating her Texas drawl for effect, she greeted rivals by saying, "Yep, I'm going to beat you," or "OK, Babe's here! Now who's gonna finish second?" After a good shot she'd compliment herself: "Ain't that pretty?" She even taunted men she beat: "Don't you men wish you could hit a ball like that? And me just a little old gal!"

Her self-promoting ways were seen as obnoxious and childish by some (especially those who believed women were supposed to pretend they weren't very good at anything), but she was also being practical. Mastering publicity helped her career—and her teasing knocked opponents off balance.

Equally good at turning fame into financial reward, she would wheel and deal to get meals and hotels for free. She offered to have a photo taken of herself with a store owner in exchange for a Rolex watch. "Hey, I'm gonna *get* me one of those," she said when she saw an item she liked. A fast driver, she bought increasingly costly cars as she grew richer.

Zaharias was often torn between her glamorous and demanding schedule and her desire to be a homebody. After a tournament she liked to return to her hotel and hop into her pajamas, and she often expressed a desire to get back to her pots and pans. Toward the end of her life she built her dream house in Florida, inspired by ideas she had written on slips of paper over the years about things she had admired in other people's homes. Called Rainbow Manor, it was on the end of a golf course and overlooked a small lake. She had a poodle named Bebe, two cocker spaniels, and three deep freezers for the food that companies were always giving her. She claimed her "beauty diet" consisted of eating anything she wanted, except gravy and other greasy fare. Favorite foods included pork and beans, onion sandwiches, strawberry sodas, banana candy, chili, and buttermilk.

When sportswriters named Zaharias the Greatest Female Athlete of the First Half of the Twentieth Century, she set a goal of conquering the second half as well. But in 1953 she was diagnosed with terminal colon cancer. Doctors told her she would never play golf again, but fourteen weeks after painful surgery (she kept golf clubs in her hospital room and sometimes even in her bed), she was back on the course.

Within a year she regained her top position and was using her prominence to educate people about cancer. At a time when the topic was considered unmentionable, she talked openly; after a victory she would say, "This should show people not to be afraid of cancer." She did fund-raising for cancer research and whenever possible visited cancer patients, playing harmonica for them and talking. As with other problems she had confronted, she said, "When you get a big setback like that, there's no use crying about it. . . . You just have to face your problem and figure out what to do next."

Zaharias had a relapse and died at age forty-five. President Dwight Eisenhower opened his news conference that day by saying, "I think that every one of us feels sad that finally she had to lose this last one of all her battles." Known by then as a humanitarian as well as a major sports hero in an age when all such heroes were male, Zaharias had permanently changed the relationship between women and sports in the United States.

Athleticisms

At age twenty-one, at the tryouts for the 1932 Olympics, Zaharias competed as a "team" of one. In a three-hour span she won five events, tied another, and finished fourth in another. Her performance was called the most amazing in track-and-field history for either men or women, and Zaharias always remembered it as one of the most thrilling times in her life. (In second place was a team of twenty-two women.) At the Olympics she was allowed to enter only three events—hurdles, javelin, and high jump—and won two gold medals and one silver.

Of all the sports she was good at, Zaharias decided to focus on golf because it was one of the few areas where women could have a professional role. She memorized the rule book and went to the course at 5:00 A.M., practicing as much as sixteen hours a day. Sometimes she hit fifteen hundred balls in a row, bandaging her hands when they became bloody or blistered. In her first championship game, the enthusiastic crowd knocked her flat into muddy water. But she won anyway and was proclaimed in the papers the next day to be "the most promising woman golfer in the U.S." She went on to win a total of eighty-two tournaments.

Sonja Henie

BORN IN 1912 AND DIED IN 1969
IN OSLO, NORWAY

*Norwegian American figure skater who
was the world champion for ten years in a row,
the dominant figure in her sport*

SONJA HENIE had a love affair with speed—a life without whirling was just "colorless" and "pointless." Whirling from place to place and challenge to challenge, she won her first ice-skating contest at age five; the prize was a little silver knife that she kept under her pillow for luck before important competitions. While developing nineteen types of spins (some of which required whirling eighty times), she worked herself so hard that she said her muscles felt electrified; at night she was too exhausted to move. As the youngest world champion in figure-skating history, she brought skating—previously a sport for the very rich or for people in countries with plenty of natural ice—to the attention of masses of people worldwide.

Being a movie star was another early childhood dream, and Henie pursued it aggressively, moving to Hollywood after her last Olympic competition and signing a lucrative contract to appear in movies as a skating actress. To reach her goal of being a number one box office attraction, she got up each morning at five, worked a twelve-hour day, and went to bed early. She had massages twice daily, and on Sunday she tried to catch up on sleep. Raw eggs and raw beef were staples of her diet. She brought leftovers home to her Norwegian elk hounds, Tonja and Heika, and several tiny poodles. Between movies she resumed her love affair with speed—the ice show in which she starred toured the world, drew record crowds, and caused riots, breaking new ground in entertainment during a pre-TV era.

A shrewd businesswoman, Henie had a second, more concrete love. She was a millionaire by age twenty-six and eventually earned $50 million—making her a contender for distinction as the richest athlete of all time. She married three times, also to millionaires. She rode in white Rolls Royces, wore white dresses, and was so glittery with jewels that she reminded people of a Christmas tree. A magazine once ran a story entitled "Is Sonja Henie Money Mad?" Possessions were important to her; when a burglar broke into her hotel room and stole two furs, she chased him down an alley in her nightgown.

Henie spent summers in a home she built on a wooded island off the Norwegian coast, and in Hollywood she lived in an elegant Spanish-style mansion on five acres. She had a maid, cook, secretary, chauffeur, hairdresser, and the constant help of her parents and brother. She threw splashy parties—erecting a circus tent over the tennis court, chartering a plane to have orchids flown in from Hawaii, decorating her pool with live swans and water lilies, serving elaborate food and drink. It would take guests days to get over their headaches after one of her parties.

Henie could be generous; she sometimes treated groups of orphans to her shows and after movies would present each of her supporting skaters with a cashmere sweater or some other expensive gift. She loved gossip and had people collect it for her. She demanded perfection from those around her but couldn't stand to be upstaged. She never felt sorry for herself and detested those who wallowed in self-pity. When she was under stress she lost her temper and yelled in both Norwegian and heavily accented English. Once when she was furious with her second husband, she hired moving vans and stripped his house of all furniture, including the curtains.

Henie died of leukemia at age fifty-seven. Her will revealed that she had disinherited everyone in her family except her third husband, and at his death the money went to her foundation in Oslo. There a museum dedicated to Henie displays her art collection and a portion of her 1,470 trophies—and the little silver knife she won at age five.

Athleticisms

At her very first Olympics, in 1924, Henie finished in last place; she was only eleven. Though disappointed, she was confident that she would improve and went on to become the skating star of the 1928, 1932, and 1936 Games—the sport's only three-time Olympic champion.

Henie's worst fear was of falling on the ice, but in reality she had nerves of steel and fell so seldom that it was big news when she did. Whenever she fell she went right back on the ice; she never missed a performance. It was important to her to appear businesslike at all times, neither worried nor arrogant.

A GLASS OF WATER ON HIS HEAD

Jesse Owens

BORN IN OAKVILLE, ALABAMA, 1913
DIED IN TUCSON, ARIZONA, 1980

*Legendary African American track-and-field star
of the 1936 Olympics in Germany*

JESSE OWENS adapted to life in his small southern town—where blacks had no rights, legal protection, or educational opportunities—by always acting pleasant around the frequently hostile white majority. By the time he moved to Cleveland, Ohio, Owens was so accommodating that he even agreed with a teacher who renamed him, mistaking the child's repeated "J. C." (for James Cleveland, his real name) for Jesse.

Frail and shy, Jesse Owens had so many chronic illnesses that another teacher thought sports might help his health. Running became his favorite activity: "I loved it because it was something you could do all by yourself, and under your own power." A coach instructed him to run as though he had a glass of water on his head, and Owens learned to soar while remaining entirely serene.

The 1936 Berlin Olympics, which took place as world events were shaping into World War II, were used by Nazi leader Adolf Hitler as a demonstration of his white supremacist theories. These toppled in light of the stunning performances of American blacks, notably Owens, who won four gold medals in one of the greatest Olympic performances of all time. A symbol of democracy standing

up to the Nazis, Owens came home to instant fame and victory parades in three cities.

It proved difficult, though, for Owens to turn fame into money to support his wife, Ruth Solomon (whom he had met in junior high), and their three daughters, Gloria, Marlene, and Beverly. He headed a government program of physical fitness for blacks, worked as a playground supervisor, and at one point ran the Jesse Owens Dry Cleaning Company—its slogan was "Speedy 7-Hour Service by the World's Fastest Runner." He gave many running exhibitions and was once overheard saying he was "pretty sick of running." When times were toughest, he raced against horses for money. It was humiliating, but "you can't eat four gold medals," he pointed out.

Then, during the last twenty years of his life, Owens began giving inspirational speeches, some two hundred a year, for ever higher fees. A former stutterer, he became such a spellbinding speaker that people said, "You could hear a biscuit land on the floor" wherever he spoke. He bought a brand-new car every year and new houses for his parents and himself—his last was a large ranch house in Arizona. He dressed immaculately and expensively and indulged his daughters in whatever dolls and toys and jewelry they wanted. Well liked, he was famous for looking at the bright side, for smiling in the face of adversity. But even as a national hero, he was subjected to racism; he had trouble getting admitted to movie theaters, eating in restaurants, and staying in the same hotels as white athletes. Nevertheless, he rarely became visibly angry.

A man of many contradictions, Owens was patriotic but had a habit of not paying his taxes (which got him in trouble with the government). Though he was close to his family, he led a separate life; the only night his family could count on him being home was on his birthday. He was generous with his daughters but was never seen to hug them, didn't want them to play competitive sports, and forbade them to take jobs. He traveled around the world singing the praises of physical fitness but smoked a pack of cigarettes a day and died of lung cancer at sixty-seven.

Among the many memorials created in Owens's honor are a street named for him in Berlin leading to the Olympic Stadium and a monument in his hometown that is engraved: "He inspired a world enslaved in tyranny and brought hope to his fellow man."

Athleticisms

⤞ Many experts consider the greatest single day in the history of track-and-field to be one in 1935 when Owens arrived at a track meet in Ann Arbor, Michigan. At 3:15, 3:25, 3:34, and 4:00 in the afternoon, he broke three world records and tied another; the crowd was so stunned that at times it was simply silent. Later he had to climb out a back window to avoid getting mobbed by fans wanting to know how it felt to be the world's fastest human.

⤞ Owens said of one of his 1936 Olympic contests that "it was a million thrills packed into one"—a reporter marveled that Owens was "jumping clear out of Germany." The rumor that Hitler deliberately snubbed Owens by refusing to shake his hand, though not strictly true, made Owens seem even more of a persecuted patriot. Still, President Franklin Roosevelt would not see Owens upon his return (it would have cost him too many votes from racist citizens), though Owens did go on to meet and be honored by four other American presidents.

Jackie Robinson

BORN IN CAIRO, GEORGIA, 1919
DIED IN NORTH STAMFORD, CONNECTICUT, 1972

*Trailblazing African American
baseball star, considered by some to be
America's most significant athlete*

IT IS DIFFICULT today to imagine the bombshell impact of August 28, 1945, the day John Roosevelt Robinson signed a contract with the Brooklyn Dodgers—the first black to play on a major-league team. As with much else in America at the time, organized baseball was reserved for whites—blacks were banned.

The theme of Jackie Robinson's whole life was breaking down barriers. As the youthful leader of a club called the Pepper Street Gang, he got into trouble for going in the white sections at the movies, sitting at a forbidden Woolworth's lunch counter until someone waited on him, and doing explosive cannonballs in the public pool (which was open to blacks only one day a week—the day before the water was changed).

In high school and college Robinson concentrated on sports because he didn't see how studies could improve his career options as a black man. As the star of everything—baseball, basketball, track-and-field, football—he was fiercely sought after by coaches. In the army he organized a baseball team to help counteract bleak conditions for blacks. Afterward, though unhappy with its low salaries and harsh lifestyle, he joined baseball's Negro Leagues—the only way he could continue with baseball. It wasn't long before Dodgers manager Branch Rickey noticed his talents.

To prepare Robinson for his new job in the major leagues, Rickey and others acted out insulting scenes to demonstrate the hostility he would face and gave him a book about the life of Christ. They also asked him to take a three-year pledge of silence so he would keep his feelings about his treatment to himself.

Robinson kept his promise despite vicious taunting from opponents, hate mail and death threats from baseball fans, and laws that prevented him from going to the same hotels and restaurants as the rest of the team. Even some teammates, verbal about their belief that blacks were subhuman, wouldn't sit at the same table with him. People who knew Robinson well were aware that the stress made him nauseated much of the time; he had trouble eating and would twitch in his sleep.

What kept Jackie Robinson going? The loyalty of other blacks, the support of his family and Rickey, the way children looked up to him, his own furious drive to succeed, and an ability to keep his fiery temper under control and maintain his composure: "The most luxurious possession, the richest treasure anybody has, is his personal dignity." With great pride he called the opening day of the 1947 World Series "one of the most important moments in my life." It was the first time a black—"the black grandson of a slave, the son of a black sharecropper"— had played in a World Series.

He also knew, as he took a large part in shaping the Dodgers into a winning team, that he was making money for himself, for the team, and for baseball. And

within nine years twelve of the sixteen baseball teams had black players, with blacks gaining acceptance into basketball and football as well.

Once the three-year silent period was over, Robinson's fans admired him more than ever for saying what he thought, even talking back to players who still taunted him. When he developed diabetes and lost the sight in one eye, people wrote to him, offering their own eyes for transplant.

After his retirement, Robinson became a trailblazer in business and politics—he was an executive with Chock Full o' Nuts (a chain of fast-food restaurants) and a uniquely powerful spokesman for civil rights. With his wife, Rachel Isum (a fellow college student who became a nurse), he had three children (Jackie Jr., Sharon, and David) and built his dream house among mostly white neighbors in Connecticut.

A year after his troubled oldest son died in a car crash, Robinson died at age fifty-three of a heart attack. At his funeral Reverend Jesse Jackson called Robinson more of a chess player than a ballplayer: "He was the black knight and he checkmated bigotry. . . . No grave can hold that body down because it belongs to the ages!"

Athleticisms

➤ People who assumed that Robinson had been hired by the Dodgers merely as a publicity stunt soon discovered otherwise. For several years he was considered one of baseball's top few players; in his ten seasons with the Dodgers they won six National League pennants. He was elected to the Baseball Hall of Fame in his first year of eligibility.

➤ In 1948 Robinson was thrown out of a game for heckling an umpire. Instead of being disappointed or angry, he was thrilled, because the umpire had treated him like any other player. He called the next day's headline—"Jackie Just Another Guy"—the best he ever got.

"I MUST CLIMB SOMETHING!"
Sir Edmund Hillary

BORN IN AUCKLAND, NEW ZEALAND, 1919

New Zealand mountain climber and outdoor
adventurer who made history by climbing Mount Everest,
the highest peak in the world, in 1953

EDMUND HILLARY got used to harsh conditions early in life. Like other children in his neighborhood, he walked barefoot to school no matter what the weather. His strict parents—farmers and beekeepers—believed that every disorder was caused by overeating, for which the cure was dieting. He became reluctant to acknowledge any sickness until he was almost too weak to stand. Gym teachers told him flat out that he was physically unfit.

Hillary escaped into adventure stories and read a book a day, living in his imagination, where he was always the hero. At sixteen he went skiing; his first sight of snow intoxicated him, as did eavesdropping on the conversation of mountain climbers—all such a contrast to his boring life that he thought to himself, "I must climb something!"

Hillary began spending all his free time taking trips to the mountains. The people he climbed with were the first real friends he had, and he described fear as a friend as well. Together with Tenzing Norgay, a native Sherpa from Nepal, he eventually set out to conquer a mountain that had defeated everyone who had tried so far—Mount Everest in the Himalaya Mountains. More than five miles high, this challenge offered sheer cliffs of ice, deadly winds, waist-deep snow, bitter cold, avalanches, limited visibility, and air that lacked enough oxygen to breathe without the aid of masks and tanks. But its legendary scenery and the idea of reaching a place no human had scaled before were wildly exciting.

Besides sure footing and great stamina, the trip required courage, persistence, and confidence. Crawling and wiggling when they had to, Hillary and Norgay were sustained by soup from a Thermos, very sweet lemon water, sardines on biscuits, and tins of apricots and dates. Once at the top they shook hands formally—then threw their arms around each other. They ate a mint cake, took pictures, and left mementos (a crucifix from Hillary, offerings of chocolate and biscuits to Buddhist gods from Norgay).

Hillary became an instant celebrity. The fuss took him by surprise—he still thought of himself as a beekeeper carrying on his parents' business, and his first reaction to fame was that he'd have to get a new pair of pants to wear in public. But he discovered that he was an excellent speaker and was soon giving lectures all around the world. Within six years he had officially stopped keeping bees.

Hillary continued climbing other peaks and surmounting new challenges. One trip, sponsored by the *World Book Encyclopedia*, was a search for the mythical Abominable Snowman—a huge animal said to live in the Himalayas. Hillary's conclusion (that the creature does not exist—all he found was fur from a real animal, the Tibetan blue bear) hasn't ended the legend.

He took a break from climbing to marry Louise Mary Rose, a musician with whom he had three children. Restless around their houses (one in Auckland and a summer cottage on a cliff above the Tasman Sea), he sometimes took the family members along on his expeditions. After Louise and their youngest daughter were killed in a plane crash on their way to join him near Kathmandu, Nepal, Hillary dealt with grief by keeping busy working on a hospital. In between his adventures he had made himself responsible for building schools and bridges and finding other ways to improve the lives of his Himalayan neighbors.

Headstrong but modest, Hillary got along with almost everyone. He liked to laugh and was always curious and full of wonder. He kept a diary and wrote many books about his travels—adventure stories that have inspired people to take physical risks ever since.

Athleticisms

⧉ When he wasn't climbing mountains, Hillary walked or jogged a few miles each day. On trips he usually stayed healthier than companions, despite losing a lot of weight on a diet of local vegetables and fruits, especially bananas. He once finished a climb after breaking three ribs and another time was gored by the horns of a frightened yak. Minor problems included infected leech bites, blisters of astonishing size, and frozen nose drips. His biggest danger came from disabling altitude sickness, and his last expedition in the Himalayas, in 1981, ended in an emergency evacuation when he fell seriously ill.

⧉ Even after Hillary's success, only about one in seven of Mount Everest climbers actually reaches the summit, and more than 140 have died in their attempts. A blizzard in May 1996 caused the largest ever one-day loss of life; eight climbers perished despite their peak athletic condition and the high-tech equipment (such as satellite phones and laptop computers) that had been unavailable to Hillary.

Maurice Richard

*French Canadian record-breaking
hockey star, the hottest player of his day and
one of the leading goal scorers in history*

"LOOK OUT! Here comes the rocket!" an opposing player shouted—and Maurice was tagged Rocket Richard for the rest of his life.

At Montreal Technical High School, Richard studied to be a machinist, planning to make a living that way and to continue hockey for fun. Soon the fun— two games a night, seven nights a week—started squeezing everything else out. During his eighteen-year career with the Montreal Canadiens, he terrorized opponents with his explosive skating speed, his intensely competitive attitude, and his mere appearance. He glared so ferociously that he could immobilize opponents with a look; a player in his way once noticed that Richard's eyes were "flashing and gleaming like the lights of a pinball machine."

Richard's other trademark was perseverance—he became famous for never giving up, despite numerous injuries. Especially at first, when he spent more time off the ice than on due to broken bones, some believed him too "brittle-boned" to play. He missed hundreds of games, but whenever he came back he somehow played better than ever. He was so energetic he often had trouble sleeping, and he hated the sight of blood, particularly his own.

"I'm unpredictable," Richard once admitted. Most of the time he was quiet and aloof; during long train trips with his team he was often completely silent. Still, he could be cheerful, and he was devoted to friends and family. When his younger and smaller brother (known as Pocket Rocket) began playing on his team, Richard at first tried to protect him, until he realized that Henri didn't need it. Richard loved young fans and always carried things to hand out to them but rejected the idea of having an organized fan club: "Instead of the kids spending money on us, let us spend money on them," he said.

But his temper was appropriately rocketlike, and passion for his sport occasionally put him in conflict with those who didn't see things his way. When he was suspended from play-off games because he lost his temper and struck an official, furious fans poured into the streets and caused thousands of dollars' worth of damage in what became known as the St. Patrick's Day riot. Richard was devastated—"numb from head to toe"—and went on the radio to appeal for calm. The only award he never won was one given for good conduct.

Richard was so obsessed with hockey that he married Lucille Norchet, who was the sister of a fellow player. She missed only two games during his career and was the one who talked him out of quitting whenever he seemed jinxed by injuries. They had six children ("one for each hundred of my goals," he joked)—Huguette, Maurice Jr., Normand, Andre, Suzanne, and Paul—and lived in a large one-story house by the Black River in Montreal.

Richard retired in 1960 at thirty-nine to spend more time with his family, two years after an injury to his Achilles tendon began to affect his playing. In an unprecedented move, he was voted into the Hockey Hall of Fame after just nine months of retirement, instead of the usual minimum of five years. Many regarded him as not just an athletic hero but as a national idol, and in a 1983 Montreal newspaper poll, Richard tied for Man of the Century.

Athleticisms

➤➤ "Never have I met a man with such singleness of purpose," said one who knew Richard. The best example of his ferocious energy was the day in 1944 he spent moving furniture, including his piano, and getting settled in his new house. That night he went out and scored eight points—a record that stood for more than thirty years.

➤➤ Game seven of the 1952 Stanley Cup play-offs was said to be the most exciting hockey game ever played. After Richard was knocked unconscious by an opposing player and carried off to be stitched up, he was presumed out for the game. But, still dazed, he soon returned to the ice. Squinting through the blood oozing from the gash over his left eye, Richard scored the tie-breaking, cup-winning goal, which was followed by a four-minute standing ovation.

Maureen Connolly

BORN IN SAN DIEGO, CALIFORNIA, 1934
DIED IN DALLAS, TEXAS, 1969

*American tennis player who was the
first woman in history to win all of the world's
major tennis tournaments*

ONCE HER MOTHER finally obliged her requests for a $1.50 racquet, tennis was the focus of Maureen Connolly's life. Six years later, at age sixteen, she became the youngest champion of women's tennis in the United States and after that lost only four matches during the rest of her career. Three years in a row she was voted Female Athlete of the Year by sportswriters. Then, at nineteen, she won the "grand slam"—all four major international tournaments: Wimbledon, the French Open, the Australian Open, and the U.S. Open—the first woman to do so.

Connolly, known invariably as Little Mo because of her height (five feet three inches), sacrificed a "normal" teen life to tennis. She fit her schoolwork in between practice and travel and attended no proms or after-school activities. Instead, she attended the coronation of Queen Elizabeth II, met the pope (he asked about her tennis), played tennis with Hollywood stars, went surfing in Hawaii, strolled the sidewalks of Paris, visited Aztec monuments in Mexico, and asked soon-to-be president Dwight Eisenhower, "What did you have for breakfast?"

Connolly had two personalities. Off court, she was sweet, bubbly, and popular with crowds. She was generous in praise of others, tending to credit "Irish luck" for her own success. On court, her face became tightly drawn; she was a fierce, deadly competitor. Privately she acknowledged a hatred of her opponents, combined with a fear of losing: "The tennis court became my secret jungle and I, a lonely, fear-stricken hunter," she wrote later. "I was a strange girl armed with hate, fear, and a Golden Racquet."

Connolly wore white cotton or sharkskin tennis dresses designed especially for her. Her favorite was a fanciful creation with woolly poodles (each with a rhinestone eye) running across it in a row. She always wore two good luck charms: a heart-shaped locket bracelet from her mother and a ring in the shape of two dragons guarding a ball. To replenish her energy during games, she sucked sugar lumps and sipped hot tea with lemon. Off court she liked steak, hamburgers, and big salads. To improve her footwork, she took up ballet, tap dancing, and skipping rope in what she called a "red-hot pepper" way. She wrote a column called Letters from Little Mo for a newspaper and later did articles for magazines, in part to help pay her tennis expenses. She was not a good public speaker. Connolly tended to talk fast under normal circumstances, and when she had stage fright she sounded like a machine gun.

The second most important activity in Connolly's life was riding horses. After the glittering parade San Diego held when she returned as the top woman tennis player in the world, the Chamber of Commerce presented her with her own horse, Colonel Merryboy, her dearest wish come true. A year later the horse panicked and threw her into an approaching cement-mixing truck, crushing her right leg. Six weeks after the accident she was cautiously back on court, but the injury was more serious than she thought, and within months she announced her retirement.

The first time she had ever played tennis with Norman Brinker, once a member of the Olympic equestrian team, children on the sidelines had called out their sympathy for him. Connolly and Brinker went on to marry, and she taught tennis to people of all ages, wrote books on tennis, and had two children. Connolly was excited about living in "the center court of Babyland," but she died young, at thirty-four, of cancer.

Athleticisms

➤➤ Early in her career Connolly sometimes lost her temper on court, glaring at officials, hurling balls, and even throwing her racquet. In the shower after one such display at fourteen, she told herself that unless she could control her anger she would have no future—all her temper did was bolster her opponent's confidence. She never lost it on court again; in fact, her coach called her "the best sportsman in tennis."

➤➤ In 1952, in London for the first time, Connolly was nervous and scared. Her stormy relationship with a coach had ended bitterly; she was being treated for a painful shoulder condition; journalists hounded her day and night; and with the weight of American pride on her shoulders, the match was not going well. The crowd was tense and silent, when suddenly a young man from the U.S. Air Force yelled encouragement. Connolly took strength from that to go on to become the second youngest winner in Wimbledon history.

Roberto Clemente

BORN IN CAROLINA, PUERTO RICO, 1934
DIED OFF SAN JUAN, PUERTO RICO, 1972

*Black Puerto Rican baseball player famous
for three thousand hits—the first Latino
elected to the Baseball Hall of Fame*

ROBERTO CLEMENTE's first baseball games in Puerto Rico made use of a stick cut from a guava tree (the bat), old coffee sacks (the bases), and knotted bunches of rags (the balls). After graduating to broomstick handles and old tin cans, he was discovered by a rice company executive who was putting together a softball team for his company. Playing professionally, Clemente earned forty dollars a week at age eighteen. Eventually he was making $100,000 a year as a Pittsburgh Pirate, and by his thirtieth birthday he was driving a white-and-avocado-green Cadillac.

Somewhat superstitious, Clemente would wear the same shirt the following day for luck if his team won. Even when a winning streak lasted eleven games, as once happened, his teammates didn't complain, despite the smell. His favorite foods were rice and beans, roast pork, and a special punch he concocted to build strength—a bottle of grape juice mixed with several raw eggs. On the road he ate steak and potatoes every night and steak and eggs for breakfast. Clemente dressed more seriously than his teammates, in well-tailored suits and shirts with cuff links. He had friendships and running jokes with other players and

participated in all their card games but not in their wilder antics. On the road he read Westerns and adventure stories like *The Count of Monte Cristo*. At home he took up ceramics, making lamps he placed all around his house; he enjoyed music and taught himself to play an electric organ. Sometimes before games he sang hymns with other players.

Reporters often accused Clemente of being a crybaby, which irritated him because he had real ailments that caused him to miss many games—from back problems due to a serious car accident to malaria. During games he would concentrate so hard on catching the ball that he'd do things like dive headfirst into a concrete wall. His favorite time of the day was massage time; he got regular treatments from chiropractors and he liked to sleep a lot—"The more you rest, the prettier you become," he joked.

While picking up medicine for one of his injuries, he met Vera Zabala; she had never been to a baseball game, but he married her later that year. They had three sons and many parties in their beautiful villa overlooking San Juan. He preferred to do his own chores and repairs—another potential cause of injuries, as when he was hit by a rock while he was mowing the lawn, an incident that sidelined him for weeks.

He was always kind to fans, visited sick children in hospitals, and made his life's ambition the building of San Juan Sports City, an elaborate six-hundred-acre area for poor kids to learn from real coaches and play with real equipment.

Particularly popular in Puerto Rico, he was once presented with a congratulatory scroll signed by one of every ten people in the country. He faced discrimination for the first time in American southern cities where his hotels, restaurants, and even drinking fountains were separate from the white players'. If he felt he was being discriminated against in a store, he would argue with clerks, reveal his identity, accept their praise, and then leave without buying anything.

"*¡Arriba! ¡Arriba!*" (Spanish for "Let's go! Let's go!") fans would shout whenever it was Clemente's turn to bat—and he responded. In baseball history, only ten players had gotten three thousand hits. One cold and rainy night, Clemente joined them, at age thirty-eight, much to the delight of twenty-four thousand cheering fans.

Three months later he died on New Year's Eve in a plane crash on the way to Nicaragua to help earthquake victims. In Pittsburgh a neon sign went up that read: ADIÓS AMIGO ROBERTO. He was elected to the Hall of Fame just three months later, instead of the usual five years.

Athleticisms

➤➤ After the 1960 World Series, when the Pirates came from behind to win, Pittsburgh turned into a giant party. Clemente, rather than celebrating with teammates at the clubhouse, changed his clothes and wandered around the streets to celebrate with citizens, feeling more like a fan than a player. He had a quiet way of rejoicing. "I am very happy, but I don't have to jump up and down," he explained.

➤➤ When Clemente was named the Most Valuable Player of the 1971 World Series, he spoke on television to his mother and father: "On this, the proudest day of my life, I ask your blessing." Clemente's loyalty was famous. With his first big raise, he bought a new home for his parents, and his three thousandth hit he dedicated to the rice company executive who had discovered him.

Wilma Rudolph

African American runner who in 1960
was the first woman to win three gold medals
at a single Olympics

CROWDS IN ROME CHANTED, "Vil-ma! Vil-ma! Vil-ma!" Wilma Rudolph was shy but so appealing that, to the crowds at the 1960 Olympics, she was the most popular of the six thousand athletes who had come from all over the world.

Being there was an undeniable triumph. Only eight years before, Rudolph had been unable to walk without a brace on her left leg. Her multitude of childhood illnesses included polio, which left her leg paralyzed. Rudolph, though, was a child for whom belief made all the difference: "The doctors told me I would never walk, but my mother told me I would, so I believed my mother." Her mother made many sacrifices to get Rudolph medical treatment. At age twelve, when Rudolph was finally able to walk unaided, she made up for lost time by becoming the star of her high school basketball team.

Running, unlike rigorous basketball practice, was just "pure enjoyment," not work. "I loved the feeling of freedom in running, the fresh air," said Rudolph. She did, however, have to work at running when she was invited to join the Tiger-belles, the Tennessee State University track team. At first she lost every race she entered, but by sixteen she was not only the fastest Tigerbelle but the youngest member of the U.S. Olympic track team. Neighboring merchants got together and gave her new clothes and luggage for her first airplane journey. Her team finished in third place, but four years of intensive training later, she traveled to Rome for a second attempt. This time she ran her way to a stunning three gold medals.

Rudolph opened doors for other women in numerous ways, becoming the first woman to win several prestigious awards and to take part in competitions previously limited to men. Known variously as the Black Gazelle, the Black Pearl, and the Tennessee Tornado, Rudolph traveled the world as an honored athlete, sometimes attracting enough fans to cause riots.

Though terrified of public speaking at first—it scared her more than Olympic competition—she became good at it and was soon in great demand. When she was invited to the White House, she was astonished when President John Kennedy missed his chair and fell to the floor; laughter all around broke the ice.

Rudolph, who endured many ugly racist incidents, used her fame whenever possible to help advance the cause of civil rights.

Rudolph married Robert Eldridge, her childhood sweetheart, who had years earlier thrown rocks at her to get her attention. She had their first daughter, Yolanda (a future Tigerbelle), when she was seventeen and later had Djuana, Robert J., and Xurry. She retired from running the year she won the Babe Didrikson Zaharias award for most outstanding female athlete in the world; she signed her last pair of track shoes and gave them to a boy who had asked for her autograph. Working hard at having a normal life, she finished college, became a second-grade teacher and high school track coach, and later was a fashion model. She also established a foundation that nurtured young athletes—in gratitude for how sports had changed her, she was "trying to develop other champions."

"I just want to be remembered as a hard-working lady with certain beliefs," she once told a reporter. "I don't try to be a role model," she added, but many have seen her that way anyway. She died of a brain tumor at fifty-four.

Athleticisms

➤ All odds were against Rudolph at the 1960 Olympics. At one point during the relay race she fumbled, nearly dropping the baton passed to her by a teammate. But crowds went wild as she recovered and went on to win a gold medal—her third—thus establishing herself as "the fastest woman in history." Fellow teammates were not so enamored; some got jealous and stopped speaking to her. As a prank they hid her hair curlers, and she was forced to attend an award ceremony wearing a hood because her hair was such a mess.

➤ Gracious and kind, Rudolph carried herself like a queen. Sometimes she was too nervous before races to eat, or else got sick to her stomach, but outwardly she struck people as unusually calm and composed. She could take naps between races and once was so relaxed after an important race that she immediately fell asleep, to the surprise of her teammates.

Arthur Ashe

BORN IN RICHMOND, VIRGINIA, 1943
DIED IN NEW YORK CITY, 1993

*African American tennis champion,
the top-ranked player in the world in 1975*

AFTER ARTHUR ASHE's mother died when he was six, he was brought up under the strict discipline of his father. He graduated from college with honors—at first studying architecture, then switching to business administration when his coach pointed out that he would have more time for tennis (and all his life he was shrewd about business). Tennis took over, and Ashe became an international star. One year he played on five continents, slept in seventy-one different beds, and made 129 plane trips.

The first black to break into the all-white world of tennis, Ashe was known as a heroic figure in overcoming bigotry. His response to discrimination was to develop an attitude of "Well, I'll show them"—he even wondered if he would have had such drive and discipline if he had been white. His early tennis teachers required him to have impeccable manners on court, so that whites could never accuse him of meanness.

"I want to be seen as fair and honest, trustworthy, kind, calm, and polite," Ashe once wrote—and indeed, everyone saw him as a near-saintly figure. A considerate neighbor and attentive friend, he went out of his way to avoid embarrassing anyone. His favorite advice to kids was, "Don't do anything you couldn't tell your mother about." Did Ashe have any faults? Naturally, he was accused of being *too* nice—a "goody-goody"—and he couldn't help noticing that people tended not to laugh at his jokes. Occasionally he was portrayed as cold, but while admitting a certain aloofness, he thought "cold" was an unfair description. Detachment, he believed, was part of tennis: Nothing was more important than the ability to control one's mood in the face of a continually changing score.

Ashe met a photographer, Jeanne Moutoussamy, at a benefit for the United Negro College Fund. She asked if she could take photos of him, he took a mental picture of her, and later they married and had a daughter they named Camera. A devoted father, Ashe read Camera to sleep every night, and the first time she read him an entire book, he cried. They lived in a luxurious Manhattan apartment and had a second home in Miami. Every Christmas Day he took Camera to visit families that were less fortunate, and they gave away toys, including a few of her own new ones. He always traveled with lots of books and magazines and as many as sixty-five cassettes of all types of music, from Beethoven and gospel to jazz and the Russian Red Army Chorus. After once losing a match when he'd had pancakes for breakfast, he never again ate pancakes or

French toast on the day of a match. He had a small wardrobe—at the end of his life, he owned only five suits and five pairs of shoes—but he bought the best quality.

Despite his international fame and wealth, Ashe felt he should be achieving more, and he became an activist in fighting social injustices. Headlines said "Negro Tennis Star Emerges from Shell" as he worked for various causes, occasionally getting himself arrested during protests. He was tempted to run for public office but ill health deterred him. After heart surgery in 1983, he contracted AIDS from a tainted blood transfusion, two years before donated blood began to be tested. Requests for him to give speeches more than tripled, and he decided not to withdraw but to publicize the realities of AIDS as best he could. He considered his most significant speech to be his address to the United Nations on World AIDS Day in 1992.

When Ashe died the following year at forty-nine, Camera was almost the same age he had been when his mother died.

Athleticisms

➤ Valuing control above all else, even in the face of insult, Ashe detested outrageous behavior on the court. The only time he was known to lose his temper was at a tournament in Sweden in 1975, when his opponent's racial taunts became "unbearable." He walked off the court, defaulting rather than responding in anger. Still, Ashe continued to consider the opponent a friend; he even attended Ashe's wedding.

➤ Ashe knew that becoming the top-ranked tennis player in the world in 1975 was supposed to be a culminating event for him, but even then he felt that his biggest mark in life was going to be made outside of tennis. In a sense he had been preparing all his life to earn this status, and on tax forms he put "professional athlete" in the box marked occupation—but after becoming just that he began to think that "the purest joy in life comes with trying to help others."

Pete Maravich

BORN IN ALIQUIPPA, PENNSYLVANIA, 1947
DIED IN PASADENA, CALIFORNIA, 1988

*The leading career and single-season scorer
in college basketball history*

PETE MARAVICH, known as Pistol Pete, believed firmly that all kids should have their long-range goals set by eighth or ninth grade. His goal? To become a millionaire. With a coach and former professional basketball player for a father, Maravich suspected his path would be basketball. Each night he hung from the door frame, believing this would make him taller, and he always carried a ball, even to movies, where he took an aisle seat so he could bounce it. He steered his bicycle with one hand so he could dribble with the other, and his family even encouraged him to dribble outside the passenger window of the car while his father drove.

Many believe that when Maravich grew up, he changed the game of basketball. For three straight years at Louisiana State University (LSU), he was the country's top scorer, averaging more than forty-four points a game. He liked to put on an exciting show and lived for the crowd's reaction—"I would feel like quitting the game if I couldn't get it. It gets in my blood." He developed tricks thought inconceivable and gave them names: ricochet drill, regular pretzel, walking pretzel, banana drill, crab catch, scrambled eggs, flapjack. In contrast to the bright white socks worn by other players, Maravich's trademark was a pair of old, sagging gray socks, which he wore for luck; he washed and dried them himself after every game.

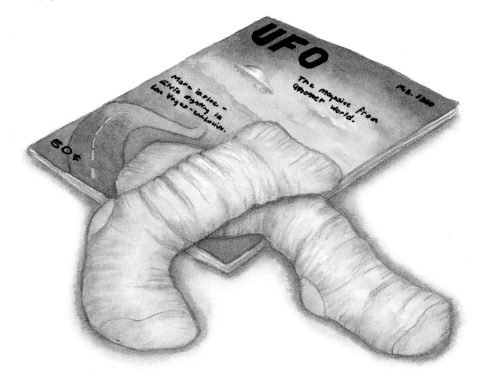

In college his dorm room was dominated by a poster of President Lyndon Johnson riding a motorcycle, dressed as a Hell's Angel. Off the court he wore jeans and LSU T-shirts and drove a tan Volkswagen. A picky eater, he did like his mother's Serbian cooking, especially her pigs in a blanket (cabbage rolls) and spaghetti with sauce that took six hours to prepare. After games he liked to go out for burgers but was sometimes delayed at the court for hours because he wouldn't leave till everyone who wanted an autograph got one.

Maravich was phenomenally popular, with reporters always following along to interview him, even when he went to the bathroom. In public he seemed easygoing, confident, and poised, but pressure sometimes got to him. Once for six months he was stricken with Bell's palsy, his nerves paralyzed on one side of his face. Away from the court he was modest, shy, and basically a loner.

After college Maravich won the most lucrative basketball contract for a rookie to date (thereby reaching his eighth-grade goal) but was plagued by a knee injury and problems with alcoholism. Searching for a cure for his unhappiness, he became obsessed with UFOs and karate, explored Eastern religions and astrology, and built his own bomb shelter. After retirement in 1980 he went into seclusion for two years. Waking one morning to hear a voice say, "Be strong. Lift thy own heart," caused him to become an active born-again Christian. He became a vegetarian; devoted himself to his wife, Jackie, and sons, Joshua and Jaeson (with whom he lived in an old country home that they restored); and started teaching at camps where kids studied nutrition, religion, and basketball (using *Homework Basketball,* a video of his dazzling moves).

Maravich was inducted into the Basketball Hall of Fame in 1987. A year later, while playing basketball with friends on a church court, he collapsed. His last words were "I feel great," but at forty he had suffered from a rare, undetected heart condition that kills most people much earlier.

Athleticisms

➤➤ Maravich spent most of his thirteenth year in an old wooden YMCA gym, almost always alone, practicing. But the pressure of making the high school team when he was only in eighth grade gave him nightmares. After the team lost the first game, he spent all night crying. A few games later he scored forty-two points and acquired his Pistol nickname from headline writers.

➤➤ Maravich tried out for the U.S. Olympic basketball team but, to most people's shock, failed to make it. Although he showed no frustration, others felt the decision was unfair. On the last day of the tryouts, when it was obvious that he hadn't played enough to show how good he was, he went out on court for a warmup and became a clown, putting on a stunt-filled show that spectators never forgot.

Bruce Lee

BORN IN SAN FRANCISCO, CALIFORNIA, 1940
DIED IN HONG KONG, 1973

*Chinese American martial artist
of legendary skill, the major influence on the
growth of martial arts in the West*

BRUCE LEE WAS BORN, according to the Chinese zodiac, during the Hour of the Dragon in the Year of the Dragon. His birth took place during an American tour of Hong Kong's Cantonese Opera Company, in which his father was a comic actor. Known in the family as Little Dragon, Lee was actually sickly and weak; he took up martial arts as a means of self-protection around his tough neighborhoods and soon became agile and versatile. A year after being named the Hong Kong Cha-Cha Champion at eighteen, he returned to the United States, where he studied philosophy and medicine.

On the side, Lee mastered every physical technique of fighting, becoming almost supernaturally good. Eventually he was most often either working out, thinking about it, or teaching others. On the street he practiced kicks on trees and pieces of litter. At the dinner table he chopped at the empty chair next to him; while watching TV he did very slow sit-ups, and even in his sleep he would kick and punch. At parties he did one-finger push-ups and would gladly remove his shirt to show off his "muscles on top of muscles." He believed that concentration was

50 percent of a workout, and "Meditation and Mental Training" always topped his daily to-do list.

Lee married Linda Emery, one of his students at his kung fu studio. Their first date was dinner atop Seattle's Space Needle. They had two children, Brandon and Shannon, and a Great Dane, Bobo, that guests weren't fond of because he drooled constantly. In restaurants Lee usually ordered two meals at once, his favorite choice being beef with oyster sauce. He drank chrysanthemum tea and high-protein drinks that he made in the blender, and consumed massive doses of vitamins, herbs, and liquidized steaks. He considered himself a sharp dresser, liked silk suits, and ironed them himself.

The word people used most often in describing Lee was *intense*; he was notoriously impatient except when talk turned to martial arts. He laughed at his own jokes, and he had an annoying habit of singing to himself on car trips. Many people also saw him as a kind and compassionate man who did favors for people he didn't even know.

Deciding that film was the best way to dispel martial arts' reputation as glorified street fighting, Lee began making his own movies, with himself as the writer, star, director, and choreographer of the fights. In the United States his movies included *Fists of Fury, Return of the Dragon*, and finally *Enter the Dragon*, considered one of the most commercially successful films ever made. Many assumed that the fight sequences used a stuntman or other tricks, but in fact Lee did his own stunts—and was forced to slow down his movements because they registered only as a blur on camera. The highest paid actor in the world, he inspired generations of Americans to take up martial arts. He had a mansion in Hong Kong surrounded by an eight-foot stone wall topped with broken glass and spikes; every room was kept locked to guard against theft by workmen.

Lee planned to retire at thirty-five, to spend more time with his family and do something beneficial for society, but he died at thirty-two from a swelling resulting from fluid on the brain. For someone in such superb condition to die abruptly was so strange that rumors have flown ever since. One claims that, like Elvis Presley, Lee is still alive and waiting to return to public life. But his body is buried in Seattle—next to that of his son, Brandon, who also became a movie actor and died suddenly, in 1993 at age twenty-eight, after being accidentally shot during the filming of a violent movie called *The Crow*.

Athleticisms

➤➤ Lee's breakthrough to fame occurred in 1964 with his kung fu performance at the Long Beach International Karate Championships. His show of precision, speed, and power attracted much attention, including that of a producer who signed up Lee for the role of Kato, the faithful aide in the TV series *The Green Hornet*. Kung fu, virtually unknown until Lee used it in combating his TV villains, became all the rage, especially with kids.

➤➤ Lee was extraordinarily single-minded about becoming a martial artist without peers. In addition to acquiring nearly every book about every type of hand-to-hand fighting, he also collected books on the benefits of positive thinking. In 1969, at one of the lowest points in his life, he wrote a statement called "My Definite Chief Aim," in which he vowed to make $10 million. Within two years this vow began to become a reality, and in 1993 the paper on which he wrote it sold for $29,000 to the Planet Hollywood chain of restaurants.

Pelé

*Brazilian soccer superstar—
the most popular player of the most
popular sport in the world*

NO ONE, INCLUDING Edson Arantes do Nascimento, knows how he got the nickname Pelé or what it means. But soon after he began playing professionally at fifteen, earning seventy-five dollars a month, his became *the* name in soccer.

Until then Pelé's life had been marked by poverty. His very first soccer ball had been a grapefruit, and his second was an old sock stuffed with newspapers. He had quit school in the fourth grade to dedicate himself to soccer.

With his ready smile, Pelé had a way of acknowledging his own talent while still seeming humble. He sometimes faced prejudice as a black man but for the most part received star treatment. The queen of England invited him to Buckingham Palace; Presidents Richard Nixon and Gerald Ford picked his brain for soccer tips. Nigeria and Biafra once declared a three-day truce in their war so that Pelé could play games in both countries—fighting resumed as soon as he left. In China, border guards put down their submachine guns (an offense they could have been shot for) to shake his hand. He received thousands of marriage proposals from fans and, as the person paying the most money in taxes in Brazil, many special privileges from the government. A shrewd businessman, he nonetheless turned down enormous sums to endorse products involving tobacco or liquor, aware of his influence on young people. Instead, there were Pelé pajamas (with AstroTurf on the soles of the feet), the Pelé computer, Pelé rubber bands, and a line of Pelé clothes that included boxer shorts.

With some, Pelé had a reputation as a moody loner, but actually he just treasured his privacy. Besieged by fame and by those who treated him almost as a religious figure, Pelé married Rosemarie Cholby, a filmmaker and photographer, and made their three-story mansion in Santos a sanctuary. Protected from nosy neighbors and fans by an Alsatian guard dog named Black, armed bodyguards, and a twenty-feet-high circular wall, the estate included a forty-seat movie theater, a photo lab, an oval swimming pool, a sauna and two massage rooms, a private soccer field where he could play with his three children (Edinho, Kelly, and Jennifer), a garage for four cars (a Mercedes, two Volkswagens, and an Opel), and a trophy room that contained a case of gold and jeweled knives given to him by Arab sheikhs. Business was never conducted at his house but at his purple-and-white office in Rio de Janeiro, with a patio outside where he served Café Pelé, his own brand of coffee.

People described Pelé as a gentleman, a good listener, generous (especially with charities for Brazilian children), and always on time. A careful dresser, he bought black brocade silk suits and soft sheepskin jackets in various colors. He always ate steak before games, and he cried at significant moments in his life—when he found out he was going to be a father, after he scored his one thousandth goal (the crowd's demonstration over this impossible feat lasted eleven minutes), and during the last game he played for Brazil. An avid record collector, he also played the guitar and had thirty of his songs published. He loved to fish and once caught two sharks from a hotel room window.

Too poor to afford sports equipment as a child, Pelé was worth $10 million when he retired in 1971. In accepting another $5 million a year to play an additional three years for the New York Cosmos in 1975, he wanted to boost soccer in the United States, the one country where it was not particularly popular. Today it is second only to basketball as the most popular sport for American kids younger than twelve.

Athleticisms

➤➤ During the 1958 World Cup competition, when Pelé was seventeen, he scored a goal that was talked about for years. He had sat out the first games because of an injury, only to come back and score the only goals in Brazil's World Cup victory. One was an amazing sort of "bicycle" kick backward; this was the day the Pelé legend began. Since then more people have seen him play soccer than have watched any other athlete in any other sport. Worldwide, more than ten times as many people watch soccer's World Cup competition as watch football's Super Bowl.

➤➤ To try to account for why he was unquestionably the best soccer player in the history of the sport, doctors at one point performed medical tests on Pelé. They found, among other attributes, that he had unusually keen peripheral vision and a genius IQ. As an adult, realizing the importance of education, he completed high school and college, finding geometry and playing chess particularly helpful to his game.

Flo Hyman

born in Inglewood, California, 1954
died in Matsue, Japan, 1986

*Famous African American
volleyball player who led the U.S. team to
a silver medal in the 1984 Olympics*

ALMOST ALL HER LIFE Flora Jean Hyman towered over others. At school, being more than a foot taller than classmates led to constant jeers and unfunny nicknames like the Jolly Green Giant. Her first instinct was embarrassment, and for a while she tried camouflaging herself by slouching. But her mother, who was also tall, talked her out of that. "Either you benefit from being tall or you hide," Hyman commented years after she had chosen a way to benefit: by joining Morningside High School's volleyball team.

Hyman's parents weren't athletes (her father worked for the Southern Pacific Railroad, and her mother cleaned houses until she had the money to open her own café, the Pink Kitty), but her two older sisters were active volleyball players. Family members called her Floey, and to others she became known as Flo, one of the best volleyball players in the world.

On a volleyball scholarship to the University of Houston, she majored in math and physical education, then postponed finishing college to pursue volleyball. "You can go to college any time, any day. You can only do this once," she decided in her usual no-nonsense manner. A self-described klutz at first, she conducted her sixteen-year career with elegance and flair. Opposing players flinched at the prospect of being near when she spiked the ball—not only was she six-feet-five but she could propel herself several feet higher and make a ball sound like a firecracker when she struck it.

Her first reaction to finding out that volleyball was a sport at the Olympics was determination to make the U.S. team. Indeed, her skill moved women's volleyball from obscurity to international acclaim. In 1976 the U.S. women's team failed even to qualify for the Olympics, but three years later, with Hyman on the team, it was ranked second in the world. When she guided the team to its first medal ever, the matches were so exciting that volleyball received some of the highest TV ratings of the Olympic events.

Hyman called herself the old lady of her teams because she was often the oldest player. Others saw her as friendly, gracious, and the hardest worker they had ever seen. She spent most of her time in the gym, practicing six to eight hours a day, six days a week. If a team got three weeks off for Christmas, Hyman would take

one, then practice on her own the other two. She had her own apartment, and except for occasional excursions out dancing or to the movies, she liked to live quietly. Besides volleyball, her other passion was reading historical romances; she would splurge on five at a time in bookstores.

After the Olympics, with no opportunities for professional volleyball in the United States, Hyman joined a Japanese league. During one match against a team that her team had never beaten, she was substituted out of a game. She turned to shout encouraging words to teammates, sat down on the bench near her coach, and closed her eyes. A victim of Marfan's syndrome—a rare, hard-to-diagnose heart disorder disproportionately affecting tall people—she was dead at age thirty-one. Her team kept playing and ended the other side's eighty-eight-game winning streak.

A year later Hyman was inducted into the Volleyball Hall of Fame, and the Women's Sports Foundation established the Flo Hyman Award for the athlete "who captures Flo's dignity, spirit, and commitment to excellence."

Athleticisms

➤ As a ninth grader Hyman made the high school varsity team after her sisters asked the principal to bend the rules. But being the youngest player was intimidating—she showed up for the first day of practice, looked around, and walked out. It was the only time Hyman was known to have sidestepped a challenge. The following year was a different story, and the year after that she was voted the team's Most Valuable Player.

➤ Teammates were important to Hyman. The one and only time she thought of quitting volleyball, it was because she didn't like the people she was playing with. (When her brain kept saying, "Oh, I want to play, I want to play, I want to play," she realized quitting was not the answer.) As many awards of her own that she won, she was proudest of her team's Olympic medal—"To me, individual awards aren't important," she said.

Selected Bibliography

Arnold, Caroline. *Pelé: The King of Soccer*. New York: Franklin Watts, Inc., 1992.

Ashe, Arthur, with Frank Deford. *Arthur Ashe: Portrait in Motion*. Boston: Houghton Mifflin, 1975.

Ashe, Arthur, and Arnold Rampersad. *Days of Grace: A Memoir*. New York: Alfred Knopf, Inc., 1993.

Associated Press. *The Sports Immortals*. Englewood Cliffs, New Jersey: Prentice-Hall, 1973.

Baker, William J. *Jesse Owens: An American Life*. New York: The Free Press, 1986.

Bernotas, Bob. *Jim Thorpe: Sac and Fox Athlete*. New York: Chelsea House Publisher, 1992.

Biracree, Tom. *Wilma Rudolph*. New York: Chelsea House Publisher, 1988.

Brennan, Joseph L. *Duke: The Life Story of Duke Kahanamoku*. Honolulu: Ku Pa'a Publishing Inc., 1994.

Cayleff, Susan E. *Babe: The Life and Legend of Babe Didrikson Zaharias*. Urbana, Illinois: University of Illinois Press, 1995.

Cohen, Neil, editor. *The Everything You Want to Know about Sports Encyclopedia*. New York: Bantam Books, Inc., 1994.

Connolly, Maureen. *Forehand Drive*. London: MacGibbon & Kee, 1957.

Creamer, Robert W. *Babe: The Legend Comes to Life*. New York: Simon & Schuster, 1974.

Davis, Mac. *100 Greatest Sports Feats*. New York: Grosset & Dunlap Publishers, 1964.

Falkner, David. *Great Time Coming: The Life of Jackie Robinson, from Baseball to Birmingham*. New York: Simon & Schuster, 1995.

Gaffney, Timothy R. *Edmund Hillary: First to Climb Mount Everest*. Chicago: Childrens Press, 1990.

Gallico, Paul. *The Golden People*. Garden City, New York: Doubleday & Company, Inc., 1965.

Grange, Red, with Ira Morton. *The Red Grange Story: An Autobiography*. Urbana, Illinois: University of Illinois Press, 1993.

Henie, Sonja. *Wings on My Feet*. New York: Prentice-Hall, Inc., 1940.

Hillary, Sir Edmund. *Nothing Venture, Nothing Win*. New York: Coward, McCann & Geoghegan, Inc., 1975.

Hollander, Phyllis. *100 Greatest Women in Sports*. New York: Grosset & Dunlap Publishers, 1976.

Johnson, William, and Nancy Williamson. *"Whatta-Gal": The Babe Didrikson Story*. Boston: Little, Brown & Company, Inc., 1977.

Lee, Mike, and Jack Vaughn, editors. *The Legendary Bruce Lee*. Santa Clarita, California: Ohara Publications, Inc., 1986.

Lipsyte, Robert. *Jim Thorpe: 20th-Century Jock*. New York: HarperCollins Inc., 1993.

Lipsyte, Robert, and Peter Levine. *Idols of the Game: A Sporting History of the American Century*. Atlanta, Georgia: Turner Publishing, Inc., 1995.

Maravich, Pete, and Darrel Campbell. *Heir to a Dream*. Nashville, Tennessee: Thomas Nelson Publishers, 1987.

Marcus, Joe. *The World of Pelé*. New York: Mason/Charter Publishers, Inc., 1976.

Onyx, Narda. *Water, World, and Weissmuller: A Biography*. Los Angeles: Vion Publishing, 1964.

Robinson, Jackie, with Alfred Duckett. *I Never Had It Made*. New York: G. P. Putnam's Sons, 1972.

Sherrow, Victoria. *Wilma Rudolph: Olympic Champion*. New York: Chelsea House Publisher, 1995.

Smelser, Marshall. *The Life That Ruth Built: A Biography*. Lincoln, Nebraska: University of Nebraska Press, 1975.

Sports Illustrated, editors. "Sports Illustrated's Forty for the Ages: 1954–1994." New York: Sports Illustrated Television, 1994.

Strait, Raymond, and Leif Henie. *Queen of Ice, Queen of Shadows: The Unsuspected Life of Sonja Henie*. New York: Stein & Day Publishers, 1985.

Thomas, Bruce. *Bruce Lee: Fighting Spirit*. Berkeley, California: Frog, Ltd., 1994.

Vecchione, Joseph J., editor. *The New York Times Book of Sports Legends*. New York: Times Books, 1991.

Wagenheim, Kal. *Clemente!* New York: Praeger Publishers, Inc., 1973.

Walker, Paul Robert. *Pride of Puerto Rico: The Life of Roberto Clemente*. San Diego, California: Harcourt Brace & Company, 1988.

Wheeler, Robert W. *Jim Thorpe: World's Greatest Athlete*. Norman, Oklahoma: University of Oklahoma Press, 1979.

Woolum, Janet. *Outstanding Women Athletes: Who They Are and How They Influenced America*. Phoenix, Arizona: Oryx Press, 1992.